NOT IN NIGHTINGALE COUNTRY

ALSO BY JUDITH TAYLOR:

Earthlight (Koo Press, 2006)
Local Colour (Calder Wood Press, 2010)

As editor/contributor:

Meeting Points (Lemon Tree Writers, 2006)
The Tide Breathes Out (Lemon Tree Writers, 2006)

As contributor:

Sex & the City (Koo Press, 2006)
There's A Poem in My Soup and *There's A Bairn in My Broth*
(Koo Press / Books and Beans, 2007 & 2008)
Split Screen, ed. Andy Jackson (Red Squirrel Press, 2012)
Whaleback City: Poems from Dundee and its Hinterlands,
ed. W. N. Herbert and Andy Jackson
(University of Dundee Press, 2013)
Double Bill, ed. Andy Jackson (Red Squirrel Press, 2014)
New Boots and Pantisocracies,
ed. W. N. Herbert and Andy Jackson,
(Smokestack Books, 2016)
Scotia Extremis, ed. Andy Jackson and Brian Johnstone
(Luath Press, 2017)

Not in Nightingale Country

Judith Taylor

Poems

First published in the UK in 2017 by Red Squirrel Press
www.redsquirrelpress.com

Designed and typeset by Gerry Cambridge
www.gerrycambridge.com

Cover image: eva_mask/shutterstock.com

A CIP catalogue record is available from the British Library.

ISBN: 978 1 910437 69 8

Red Squirrel Press is committed to a sustainable future.
This publication is printed in the United Kingdom by
Imprint Digital using Forest Stewardship Council
certified paper.
www.imprintdigital.co.uk

Contents

for HCS

Incomer

You can play that cello all you like
to the cool, thickening dark
—nothing will answer.
The woods at the end of your garden
are low and leaning, shaped by gales
and gripping stone for a footing.
They are never heady with wild flowers.
You're not in nightingale country.

Take in your elaborate music-stand
—the dew will rust it—
close the patio doors, and light the light.
Don't be disheartened. You've been out
asking the wrong questions:
everyone does, at first. But listen later
when your neighbour makes
another midnight effort to get finished

whatever ramshackle thing he's building now.
A tawny owl will come to a near tree
and hoot the noise of his hammer back
in the same rhythm precisely, blow for blow.
Though whether in love or mockery
or to warn him off ancestral ground
I doubt we'll ever know.

A Visit from the Fiend-Like Queen

Grua happens to drop by at coffee-time
again. I think she's lonely
with Himself away subduing the North.
Caithness is a full-time job these days

and the child's gone with him this time.
Lulach adores his stepdad, she enthuses
and I nod and smile, though I think
that boy's too easily led:
no wonder they call him simple.

I offer scones. She accepts hers
with a gracious gesture
—never one to let you forget
her grandad was a king—
but she butters it thickly, wolfs it
straight down. *I like it here,* she says

away from those bloody waiting gentlewomen.
Then she remembers her manners:
but you must come round
to ours next time!
I nod and smile. She means it
but it isn't going to happen.

And I don't mind: I took a tour of Dunsinane
last Open Day. It's a draughty place.

She asks about my riding-lessons
—a subject she finds easier
than poetry, or my Dad's health—
and although I know from the morning paper
what she's been up to lately
I ask her, for the sake of politeness:

How are the re-afforestation projects going?
Just the other week she was telling the *Herald*
how she enjoys getting her hands dirty;
how good it is to be bringing native species back

to Birnam Wood.
Here, in the privacy of my kitchen
she rolls her eyes, and helps herself to another scone.
My dearest chuck. Don't ask.

Islands

Her husband was a keeper on the Skerries
(this was twenty years ago,
before they automated all the sea-lights)
and for the love of him
she had spent her whole married life on islands

exasperated. All their, *Well,*
if it doesn't come on the next boat
it'll maybe come on the boat after drove her wild;
not the slowness only,
but the way they all accepted it

as if it was like the weather, something
nobody could change. Oh, she'd tried,
but it was useless. They did it to annoy her, she decided,
or they'd all gone simple-minded
from waiting till tomorrow for today's paper.

All the while, her husband took the quiet-spoken calm
that so moved her heart when they first met
away for weeks at a time, so he could spend it
on his lighthouse,
and the boats going slowly by:

probably just as well, though, since quiet-spoken calm
was all around her now, and reduced her
to grinding her teeth. Her solace
was imagining his retirement, and a nice flat
in a red sandstone tenement on the South Side of the city;

in the meantime, she wrote home to her sister. Things like,
Send me a head for my sweeping-brush.
If I order one from the shop here
it'll take forever to come, and they just laugh at me
behind my back, when I chase them up. The replies came
slowly, on the boat.

examination

all I remembered after was the distance
from the doorway to the instrument

and light from the enormous semi-circular windows
shining off the parquet
unevenly, in the places it was broken

chairs and stands and forgotten things in corners
and how far it was to walk
out, watching my step

to walk back afterwards
to the doorway and the stone stair

and in between there was nothing

in the part I would be questioned on
there was nothing I remembered

Visitors

I said, *you can always tell when there are dolphins off the harbour*
by the boatload of marine biologists tailing them. I meant the visitors
not to hope too much that they would see them. I expect
luck of that kind to be rare now

like the small tortoiseshell butterflies,
the sparrows. As I said it though, we saw a fin: stopped the car.
There were three—two and a young one, maybe—turning lazily,
  breaching
through the grey light on the water by the coastguard station.

Cormorants overflew them;
common terns came spearing down on sand-eels by the near shore;
the sun went into a cloud behind the city. We watched a long time.

It surprised me how relieved I was to see them. Lucky again,
  this once
and not a boat of biologists in sight. Only a couple of supply-ships
going out to rigs; another coming in.

The Lapland Woman and the Finland Woman

They're peripheral to the story
grotesque beside the beautiful Prince and Princess
or the Snow Queen in her white sleigh

and even the talking ravens have more glamour
but the older I get, the more I think about
those two sisters

who live in the cold North
in houses that are always hot, since they're always cooking up
whatever they need

in the way of soup, or spells.
Hardy and self-reliant
hospitable, too, to passing strays

generous with their stores and their directions
and terribly wise:
they are the ones I want to be

not Gerda. Though I never will.
And they'd laugh to think I admire them.
They laugh more than is dignified, and don't care

who overhears.
They send each other letters
now and then, written on stockfish

and each one chuckles knowledgeably
over the other's latest
as she adds it to the pot.

Syrup

winter soon   and candying
    oh, the extravagance
forcing sweetness into   pale squares of melon
            yellow pineapple wedges
sweet before we started

            day four and counting
glassy   artificial   this is the change we make
  the syrup thickening
                        slow to drain

as slow to release its hold as this
  September   forcing its sweetness
into the chestnut leaves
                till they died
        flushed   feverish   sugar-
                                  poisoned

the low flame   and the crystals fade to   glass
        forced to their dissolution   just-
                                  bubbling

sweetness
        to drown the fruit
that floats now   approaching equilibrium
       with the thickening
  clear extravagance of the syrup

                                        and beyond the glass
in the dark   are all the pale squares of windows
    television   flushing them   candying
                  the winter

the counting down
          to December   as if to a clear
                          flare against the dark

          to a day flushed   feverish
drowning in   artificial
                    and the extravagance, oh
             forcing sweetness
                              soon

The Man

'Ay; or else one must come in with a bush of thorns and a lantern,
and say he comes to disfigure or to present the person of Moonshine'

—*A Midsummer Night's Dream* III.i

She wants frost at the full moon
a clear sky to see him.

Not the modern face, all cartoon sallow jollity
but the older man
the thief, with his load of thorn-twigs and his lantern

striding out
to lift respectable neighbours' laundry off the hedges.

By degrees she's getting nearer him:
his unconcern
—accused again, denying everything.

All the ways she sees him
get away with it

his illusions and his colourless cool responses.
That trick he has
of using every shadow

while he conceals his own.
She sees technique

she might find applications for:
she catches herself
admiring him, shiny bastard.
                                                  But she sees too

how you would laugh if she told you
she knows the breed of his dog.

The Water

River names are the oldest
the first things in a landscape.
So many times they simply mean *The Water.*

And the ones we tell a story about?
—they might be the names of lost gods and goddesses
we say. The chances are, in some lost language
they simply meant *The Water* too.

We come here for the mountain: we're
in awe before its grandeur.
But there's no living on mountains

—it was named for the river that grows
out of that thin burn at its foot.
It was the burn and not the mountain
brought The People

with their stone blades
their feet calloused from wandering
their lost word for the water.

Daffodils

For a while each year, the whole slope is daffodils:
the surgery and the fitness club and the petrol station
down one side of the road
and nothing but daffodils down the other

planted close together, flowering at the same time
in bands of different yellow shades
like a Dutch field in a catalogue.

Everyone looks. They can't do otherwise. Cars slow
on the road. Dogs sit down, bored
by their human's dallying. Words like *host* and *golden*
can be overheard at the bus-stop

as the wind obligingly flutters heads.
When the sun comes out
it's as if the daffodils brought it out on purpose.

It never lasts, of course. Kids make tracks
into it, picking flowers for their mothers;
some drunk goes rolling down the slope
like they did last year.

Age will sully it very soon.
In a week or two, the tender yellow petals
will turn papery; they will brown and dry. The whole slope
will be nothing but stems, old foliage, and seed-pods

and people will look away, it's so unsightly.
They will wonder when the Council's coming
to cut the remnants down.

Still, for the moment only a surly person, showing off
in their surliness, would mention time
or quote Herrick. The whole slope is golden:

the flowers wave like a golden sea.
The sun comes out, and people come out of their houses
to take photographs of the daffodils:
we all smile, and everything's as it should be.

Late landscape

I came here by a dark road
in open country.

Back in the day, there would have been crows
but I have come
from the city, and come alone.

I wait a moment
but there's nothing more to be seen.
The light will not reveal the horizon

or what remains of the road: it paints a veil
over any thing that lies before me.
I go forward

if I go, into a rich dusk
I dread, and know.
If I go.

Thought-experiment

Our bench on the hill above the sea is still there
its plaque saying *In Memory Of*
half-covered by a recent coat of creosote
and it still looks to the lighthouse on the horizon
under stars you knew the numbers of
but not the unscientific names, on principle.

Around it, things have changed. Everything changes:
it's the second law of the universe.
The bakery on the way home, that used to be open late at night
is long gone. Not a soul is out there on the dark reef
keeping the light. Somebody sees it blinking
on an instrument-panel, miles away in the city.

And some of the stars are gone, too, for certain
—light still travelling from a source
dead for a thousand years
before we ever came here. Indifferent
to who or what exists that might detect it
give it a name, or number...

sweetheart, think of this poem
if you have to, as a kind of thought-experiment.
Not a slapdash application against the wear of time
but a small demon
vigilant, and contrary to the known laws
shutting away the particles it wants to keep
from the general disorder

as if it could stop the whole shebang from running out
for the sake, just
of the visible stars, the lighthouse
and the place we used to see them.

Epithalamium

There ought to be something makeshift,
some improvised tilt, to a wedding,
like a foretaste
of the rackety tightrope dance—the swaying,
death-defying recoveries—
both participants know they're stepping into now
in front of their home crowd.

Or we hope they do: we remember others.
The ones who had the church booked
for longer, by a year, than the marriage lasted.
The ones whose Day
—which *they saw first*—was clashed with
by the Scottish Cup,

or the once-in-a-life reunion of Peter Gabriel
and Genesis at Milton Keynes
the Best Man had to be blackmailed
into giving up his ticket for.
                                        It isn't fun,
watching a big production number fall apart.
So our hearts sing for the ones who said
To hell with that, we can all dance in the garden.

Like fools, they chose the same weekend
as the Glastonbury Festival: but the night before,
in solid rain, they tracked the last available gazebo
to an *Argos* at the other end of the county.
And we all danced.

I wonder if they know, our teetering chancers,
just how fervently we hope to see them
keep that doubtful balance?
—on the wire, on walls, on the kerb,
on cracks in the pavement—dodging everything
they discover they've waltzed right into
under the circus lights
with the elephants looking on.

Siren

Even my name
makes you think of it.

Sax-o-phone—machinery
and base desire, in one.
And all your fantasies

of the low dives you hadn't the word to get into
hang around me
like the scent of a morning after:

whisky; stale tobacco;
Midnight in Paris.

I'm your only soundtrack
for seduction, and
in the cold of an empty night
your consolation prize:

a dancehall Sphinx
you flatter yourself you'd guess
if you ever stooped to try.

                                        Ah
if only you knew, Milord,
what my song shelters:

deep down
in my liquor-tinted, melancholy voice
as I take my solo

there is something stirring. Old
laughter, dark and blue as a shadow
and nobody's but my own.

Binding

Leatherbound, they need the touch
of our fingertips, our palms, and so
this ritual to assuage them: in the dimmed light
of Special Collections, customary
cotton gloves laid aside
you hand me down a volume

and I hold it as I've been trained: firmly,
not too tight.
I massage its spine thoroughly, touch
every nub of the hard cords
that keep the body together.
I work its every moving part

I let it drink in my essential oils
that will keep it supple, ready for use
beyond my time.

It's Volume I of a treatise.
You work on II
and we face a little apart

as if what we do here
is private. But I watch
the roll of your shoulder-blade
inside the cotton labcoat
and your fine hand, against
the grain of the
                                        —calfskin, is it?

I stroke the smooth covers
gently, steadily, slowly:
as if the living animal
were beneath my hand
and needed soothing. All
done, I clasp it once

(I feel a silly tenderness
for each, even the heavy and the awkward)
and I return it
to its place on the shelf, and reach for III.
A murmur
as I update you on our progress

but we work in silence
mostly, only our breathing
and the odd creak of the leather.

We have finished with the philosophers:
ahead of us lies a long stretch
of theologians

then the applied, and after them the pure
scientists. Me, I'm looking forward
beyond all these, to the poets.
I hope they will be slimmer
and easier to manipulate

but I hold that thought.
You might consider it foolish

and after all, we never open up
to where the words are. We know
if we searched inside
we would come to places we are dangerous:
where the very touch the skin
craves, would burn.

All Fools' Eve

Venus   at her preparations

        finger-food and music
                and those dark eyes.

I know she must be Venus.

            Who else would just come sauntering
        through my sleep this cool
 spring night

          and treat me as her audience
                  while she sets my house as
            her scene?

                  Archaic colours
        shellfish recipes
plucked strings.   I don't wait
                      to find out who the object is.

She gives me what she imagines is enough
        to entertain myself
                  and I drive away
drive all night.

        Towards dawn
            I stop the car at the seaside.

There are warplanes overhead
and there's a ferry
but I wake too soon to take it.

The lure

The man in charge of the boat that takes you out to the smaller
  island
where you will see the famous seabird colonies,
the chambered tomb, the geology the retreating ice left behind,
dislikes you very much
but doesn't show it. You're his livelihood now;

at the same time, you represent the law that stops him polishing
  off
the last fish his fathers didn't account for
and leaves him this undignified, indirect means
of feeding his kids.
All the way he reminds himself he can't afford

pride. But around the Point, he takes you very close
to the rusty old half-hull of the trawler grounded there
when he was a boy. They all escaped that time, but you don't know
  it:
you only see
the plates, slimy and red, and the gaps behind them

like the apertures in a skull that's just unfleshed.
You feel the tilt, as the sea
slopes toward it, drawn
down by the former life he skirts you round. The irresistible
  danger.

Kettins Phonebox

When I was young, back in the last century
—this was back before there was Twitter
before there were even mobiles—
the thing to get was a boyfriend with a car
so he could drive you out to Kettins, to the phonebox

and you could phone your friends, who were all
hanging round the phonebox at the Square
and say, *Hello. It's me.*
I'm phoning from Kettins phonebox.

The boys expected more than that, of course
from car possession. There was the usual
in the dark at the back the berry-fields
—though at least you would be dry in a car
and safe from creepy-crawlies—

and there was racing. Well
they used to call it racing
but none of the roads was wide enough
for two abreast. It was time-trials:
the Route Avoiding Low Bridge

and back to the Square.
And even that was finished
after the night Christie smashed
his car, his girlfriend and himself
into a farm wall.

As for the other
these were boys of the last generation
whose parents made them marry the girl
so nobody—boyfriends, girlfriends—
got away with anything really

and it was so little, what they wanted.
Brief acceleration
going out that road. To phone the ones
you'd left behind: *hello. It's me.*
I'm phoning from Kettins phonebox.

Vodka, orange juice, Galliano

A cocktail from my past, yellower
sweeter than I remembered

and the oily trace I used to think I detected
isn't there now, if it ever was.

No trace of the music either:
the candlelight, the beech tree scattering

small, unpretty blossom
over the grass outside the French doors.

No trace of the girl who stood
her back to the party

watching it all fall.
And why

would she have stayed, if what you remember is
the way it was?

Drink it down to the ice
and come away from the darkened window

away from the heavy river.

Flowers

I wanted to write an elegy
without flowers. I know they're a requirement

but I wanted not to think of the way we hid
the new, dark scar your grave was
under pretty coloured flowers

and little messages.
Only, what else could I speak of
in that bitter day?

                                        Nothing weather.
Trees on the edge of the river

empty, not prepared
to consider spring

and everything we had lost with you
—your bright stare, your serious smile
your dancing—

lost already
beyond the last of our hopes' reach.

I wanted not to think of the way we turned aside
and left you, as we had to
in a place where you had neither leaves nor birdsong

for shelter, only
grey grass, still keeping its winter,
and our terrible swathe of flowers.

To go on with

News comes
right at you, and you've no hope

imagining things you could have done
each of them
less plausible than the last

which is how the mind deals with finality:
scenarios. Fictions
to go on with.

I want to ask the prayers of all the saints
I don't believe in

especially those the Church
has withdrawn its credence from.

St Bee, the holy arm-ring off some long ship
St Arwell, with his thorn tree and his coracle
and above all

St Fort, in whose domain
twenty years ago, I nearly died.

Pray for us now, you saint
of making *Sandford* sound like a better place to be.
Pray for another one who couldn't quite believe it.

Look down in kindness from your green hill
with its good view of the estuary

volunteers are dragging
for a sign, for anything
while there is light.

Opera in the Park

The lords of the world are different.
They say *victory*:
you or I would say

love.
Dry your eyes.

It's ten at night on a Friday
and you have to cross Union Street
on the way home.

You'll be noticeable enough
amid the lit-up, shiny couples
without them wondering why you're crying.

And what would you say
if asked?

The beautiful bitch got him.
Not the slave, the one
who really loved him.

Flute song

I'm tired of playing the sweet girl
with the silvery, cheerful voice

the lilting bird tone
that is so reliably brightening

when I could be low
insinuating

muscular
as a serpent

my sidelong trail in the dust
your only indication

where I've been.
I could be bleak

hazardous: knives
glitter too; poisons flow.

To produce those dancing phrases
you delight in

I use force: I make
hard, disciplined air.

You know to fear me
when I'm thirty strong, with drums

—do you think all that comes out of nowhere?
Do you ever think

when you hand me another part
as a babbling ingenue

you could push your luck
too far? That you could one day ask a girl

to be just that last degree
too light, and bright, and sparkling?

Gardeners' Latin

Spring again, and the juice rises
sticky and clear in the veins of the public flowers.
Does the Council know, I wonder, what it's endorsing
with these hyacinths and narcissi?
—lust, bloodshed, runaway self-love?
I thought not.
But everywhere you look in this park's a bed
devoted to some swooningly beautiful youth
who died in lurid circumstances. Even the ground
throbs, in time to the traffic.

And farther back, in the shrubbery, are the women.
Hunted, forced in the catch-all name of love,
they underwent a different transformation. All this glory
and its withering, re-enacted every spring,
is not their after-life.
They armoured themselves
in bark and thorns; in tough, evergreen leaves:
and they endure. When the year goes down again
they'll offer the passing children
poison fruit.

Powers that be

When the sun shines
there are always those who say
they made it shine

—that they alone
know the magic words, and for this
deserve to be rewarded royally.

When the sun goes, just see
if we can catch them
owning their responsibility
in the darkness.

And this is what it is
to be one of the powerful:

you can claim the sun.
Your priesthood sings the chorus
and if other histories linger

you can have them written out,
burned;
the First Chinese Emperor did.

Like him, you take a medicine
you think will make you immortal
but that makes you in fact insane

and when you sleep at night
it's as he sleeps
in his huge tomb

protected by a loyal army of imitation soldiers
and an imitation river of
real poison.

A carved throne

In Persepolis, this piece
that stands beside the King
defending him, was a grand vizier they say
or else a general.

In Trondheim and the Outer Isles, we find
a queen on a carved throne
who seems dismayed, anxious.

We know this people had tough queens,
overrulers of their bearded kings,
implacable avengers:

if you wanted an undisturbed reign
you were best to start by packing off the old queen
—whoever she was, even your own mother—
to enforced peace in a nunnery

and here's one at the height of her power
but look at her. Her mouth clenched,
hand pressed to the side of her face,
her eyes round and staring

as the lines are drawn up yet again
and the rival king—who may even be her brother,
cut from the one tusk—stirs up the feud
her marriage was supposed to have put an end to.

Her kin will die, or her husband.
We will see her give her sons up to the flames
will see her taken
with the other chattels of victory.

All the same, when trouble comes
she'll make her moves
as boldly and as ruthlessly as any lord:

a combination of bishop and berserker
she will slice her way through hostile dispositions
to protect whatever she calls her own.

Only her face will stay
fixed, an ivory mask of horror
at what she sees before her.

Requiem

—after a sculpture by Barbara Hepworth
in Aberdeen City Art Gallery

You want to think
it's a human shape. It isn't
quite.

You want to think it's a bone flute
for the wind to play, but too much
is eroded out.

You want to think
that smooth surface resigns itself:
a ruined tree, made furniture.

You want to think its pierced places
fill with light, when the heart of it
is a pool of shadow.

You want to think.
You want some form of containment
the form itself will not give

for memory
for enduring grief.
You want an explanation.

You circle it
closer in this time.
There isn't an explanation.

Demeter reads the Scotch Encyclopaedia

It is not to be imagined
that all the stars

glimmerin bricht as diamant
on the black silk o a winter nicht

are placed in one
concave surface equally distant from us

set oot like the dawin's reid gowd
the relict warld's inheritance

a braw lowe, an comfortless
as a girnal stowed wi sand an yella stane

but that they are scattered

as the simmer burds are scattert
the flourish an aa the sma fruct o the trees

an aa the luves we kent
in oor life afore the nicht
scattert

at immense distances
from one another...

aa we possest, iver, o
hopefu', young: tint
in the maisterie o the deid pooers

no limit can be set
either to their number or their distance.

Note: Lines in italics taken from the entry for Astronomy in the first edition of the *Encyclopaedia Britannica,* published Edinburgh 1768–71

Nocturnal

There is nothing
in this fantasy:

a bright wrapping
on the old midwinter dark.

Look at us all
uneasy, all pretending

not to be tired now.
Pretending we got our wishes.

Look at the things we brought
ourselves. The packages shaped like spirits

tied up, waiting their moment
in the shadows below the tree.

Lean times

I walk the discoloured world
like a bear unable to sleep
for hunger

unable to find
sustenance under the white dust
or the grey glass it turns to.

Whoever brought this
Calvinist cold, you can stop now:
it isn't making me better

only blunt with rage
and exhaustion as I stumble
over my own tracks in the void again.

What did you think?
—by stripping everything down
you would enrich it?

Do you think those birds,
fluffed out and tremulous
on the end twig of starvation, are being

cheerful in adversity?
They don't know how.
And me, I'll live. I always do.

I'll stick my head in the garbage
at the back of your bright, insulated house;
I'll eat my own spoor;

I'll last this out, and see
whatever worse time might follow it. Only
now you've brought my anger down

where you live, don't
please
act surprised to see me use it.

Raven, Stac Pollaidh

Your black plumes
take in all the light, and yet
you shine.

The clap of your wings is
slow and so
considered

it's a wonder how the cold
wind resists you or

sustains you
as you glide
above your high lands

deliberating where
you will go to dine
today.

We see you
with the dead

and we shine our own
thought and memory
on your darkness.

Our stories give you
speech and
evil omen

yet you are gracious
and delicate
in your season

the bones of your body
so fine

it's as if you have inherited them
already stripped
and windblown.

You live so long
you learn
to mourn.

You step out
into nothingness

below the frightened walker
on the hard crag:
your voice knocks

like a warning
like the clapper
in the stone bell of your country.

Fairytale ending

She thought she wanted a daughter
white as snow
red as blood
and black as a raven.

She was given
only a counterfeit of herself.
Or at least, that's all she saw: her mirror-image

glaring back
as if at some wheedling, poisonous crone.
She knew her powers would never hold
that girl's heart

and she sensed,
wandering somewhere
out of reach, her wished-for
perfect child.

Too late, she saw
how the wish had been granted
twisted; saw the landscape
under her window shimmer again

as it had that bitter year.
They had recreated it all between them.
Injury. Claws. Cold.

For These Times

a girl can get on anywhere

I mun quit this part and try another

I only know that these people must be conquered

from birth to death
a bargain across a counter
in the main the Good Samaritan
was a Bad Economist

awlus right, and
everything to be paid for
immoral as need be

aweary of vice aweary of virtue

smoothed and varnished
any set of ideas will do

turtle soup and venison with a gold spoon

on the reasonable grounds

I'll sell thee off again, and I'll sell thee off again

used up mind apparently quite alone
and how we are awlus wrong

Note: text collaged from *Hard Times* by Charles Dickens

In Greyfriars Kirkyard

I think I'm here on a futile mission:
to find the site of the paupers' graves.
Down south, I met a Greek-American
Orthodox priest, who quoted me swathes

of 'The Great Tay Bridge Disaster'—
a McGonagall fan. Trying not to laugh,
I promised I'd find a monument
to his hero, and send a photograph.

But it seems there's nothing, here or Dundee;
a prophet unhonoured, right enough.
And he won't be up in the fancy lairs
with walls and windows and all the stuff

of property, but for a roof. Whole streets
with family names at every door—
no place for a useless poet here.
Their relatives thought them something more

than your whoreson common dead body—these walls
denote a selecter sort of clay,
though it's six feet under their founds. I ask
in the kirk. 'The paupers? I couldn't say.'

I suppose you couldn't. Well, thank-you, missus.
Fresh-cut flowers on the wee dog's grave
and the terrible bard without a name;
but then again, what inscription'll save

your memory? All the important people
up in the lairs are past recall
by now—words on a stone, flaking away.
Poets, tragedians all

in our own esteem, we're comedy
soon enough to the later living, who pass
with condescending smiles, all bound
for the same blank stone and blanket grass.

Roman Amphitheatre, Chester

There's a small room
opening off the entrance-tunnel. Bare now
but in use it would have been lamplit
its air thick
its floor sticky with offerings.

We have pretty well forgotten her
the hard goddess of getting what you asked for
cold-handedly
(if she liked your prayer) doling out
the least bad of your options.

Her sister is Fortuna, goddess of those
who read their own glossy prospectus
and believe, as if believing is the work.

Who think the casualties are self-made
and can always sell their stories:
there's no altar to her down here.

It was Nemesis—the one who laughs
now and again, but never smiles—
the working fighters prayed to
when they came to put their training
and their dumb luck to the test.

Hers was the last door they would pass by
when the word was given
—Showtime—
and they walked out into the hard light
the all-consuming roar.

The details

He keeps his paperwork resolutely
up-to-date: works on some nights
till it's finished. For it's so easy
to lose your grip on the details
then to be asked to account for something
and have to scrabble for it. None of that

in his department. Everything's logged:
arrivals, assets, relevant correspondence
and disposals, all
clearly filed. He can lay his hand
on anything you might want to know, in a second.
And he flatters himself

the smooth way the process runs out there
reflects the orderly way it's documented.
That's his contribution. Calm and order
spreading outwards from his filing-room
like light.

            No, that's too grand:
but like a benign contagion, maybe, making better
the world. He thinks himself
—will go to his grave
thinking himself—a cog, yes
but a vital one in the great machine.

He will go to his grave
resolutely thinking
he was a good man
and all he did was his duty.

The Symbolists

after graphic works by Edvard Munch

It was your friend who called her *Vampire*
and the name stuck.
You thought of him as your friend still

though he's the one who looks at you, his face
bleak as death, from every version you made of *Jealousy*

and you're the man in the background
with his wife, in conversation
under the apple-tree in the garden.

You came to regret it later
—the name, that is.
It took all ambiguity from the picture

and in fact it's just a woman
kissing a man on the neck, you said.

But it was you who gave her red hair
when you printed the colour series.

Small hours

The night is old.
It hasn't managed to stay blue:

all that is just
another thing it finds
going over the same ground.

A coloured glint
a fragment

that once held medicine, maybe.
No use for anything now though.
The night has got past the stage of

keeping pieces
even of pretty things.

It is making everything
neat and plain, prepared
for whatever's coming

though what that is, it can't
remember now.

It only know the cold
has got into its bones
the moon has taken itself away

and the stars have grown
inexplicably smaller.

uisge

the water-horse
waits in deceptive places
where the river is dark and
deeper   faster-moving
than you told yourself

though somewhere
in your memory
is a warning   never to play there

and the creature when you see it
under real or
artificial
midnight light
is all you have ever wanted

beautiful thing
your transport
anywhere
away from here

see how it shines for you
like a 4x4   a hot   hatch   the kind
left on the verge   of the dual carriageway
a night's drive
beyond the limits

body
beaten in
the little left of its windows
red
-lettered
POLICE AWARE

you know this
and all the same
you reach for it

it's not the first
to have sung you lines
you don't believe
and not the last
you imagine

it's no accident
its name on your lips like
whisky

Night driver

This is the time I like—
the hour of the friendless,

when the people who've got some place to go
are there, and safely out of the road

and we who remain can see
where they have come to, passing by us.

It's as if they leave the lights on specially,
curtains open. Sympathy? Or to ward us off with jeering?

We will never know. We drive,
each in a separate shell. We have come for this.

We can recognise our cassettes by touch
in the darkness,

ditch the radio station,
choose another one,

blind. With a tilt of the rear-view mirror
we can dim every thing

that lies behind us—all the regrets,
distances,
lights.

Ashore

Their travelling days are almost done.
He used to roam the world

and she would follow him, wherever she could:
the St Lawrence Seaway;

Mexico; Cape Town;
Hong Kong.

Today they are on the Redline bus
to the surgery. They lean together

talking discreetly all the way.
While we slump into silence, disconnected,

they observe
where the poodle parlour's moved to;

dying trees;
a block with almost every flat for sale;

the skateboard crowd
at the edge of the retail park;

a small girl in a party dress.
They are still seeing the world.

As they disembark, a plane goes over
rising slowly from the airport

and he points it out, the swallow tattoo blurred now
on the back of his freckled hand.

Where you feel it

Not in the knuckles, strangely.
The tweed protects them
from the board we knock it against:
though if we were not pretending
—if this was real—the stuff would be
soaking wet; hard and inflexible.
All our hands would be chafed raw,
the joints swollen up with the work.

A long day's labour, waulking.
Only two songs in, I can feel it
in my upper arms, that create most of the movement,
and the backs of my wrists, that keep the hands
flexed and gripping.

The singer gives us a slow one next.
Not all of this, she says,
was done at the one speed. I believe her:
but then she ups the tempo again
and says there were faster songs
for when the tweed was beginning to dry
and the work was lighter

and by now the back of my neck is complaining too
and I think, *they must have been so tired*
when they had done hours of this
it was only the end in sight,
and not the music, speeded them:
lines of women, lilting away
in grim determination
to finish the work they'd started.

Like the singer's work,
her forty years of keeping this music
fulled out, and fit to be worn
in any weather: she, too, so determined
that her language isn't about to die.

But god, she's up against it
in the memory of the weary lives
these working songs were thirled to.
Going back to my seat, the demonstration done,
I think of the old ladies, interviewed
by a folklore man, who told him
how that kind of work was gone
replaced by *all these mills and modern things.*

How sad, he said,
and one of them rose up at him
in high style. *Well, I*
think it's a good thing. It was too hard,
it was too hard for the women.

Ship to shore

He calls her from *Tranquility*
from the engine room, exasperating man he is:
at least, that's what it sounds like.

She keeps saying *I cannae hear ye*
—'Tranquility', aye, but the rest is
drooned oot. Call me back.

He calls her back,
just the same.

Oh, she knows how privacy
on a thing that size
is hard to find. But honestly: it's just
noise. He could be saying anything.

And what does he need to say now
that won't keep till he's home again?

Though even then, when she thinks about it,
it's like he needs the telly roaring, or the washing-machine
before he'll speak.

She used to think he was fearless,
out there in all conditions

and he is maybe, except for this
one thing:

the sound of his own voice, saying
—what, she can't be certain,
but it might have been *I luve ye.*

After Sappho (Fragment 22)

I beg you:
show yourself.

Tonight again the air is close
with longing

and a glimpse of you
will earth that electricity
through whoever sees.
                                        My

heart, shocked
has taken on a life of its own:

I used to sneer
at the cult of love, but now

I wish

I pray.

Fertility amulets (Roman)

Whose   dicks are you?
—trotting so perkily
with bells on   and your tails up
your blunt bronze noses up
questing towards their goal.

          How were you used?
Did someone offer you
at the right shrine?   Did she polish you
or hang you up above the bed for luck?
And how do I know   with so much certainty

that she's a *she*?   You amuse me
but to her   you could be life or death.
  A contract
is a contract: there are penalties
for those who don't deliver.

          Did she buy you
in the temple or the market?
Was she given you   by the husband
or the mother-in-law?

I see by your jaunty angle
you're as big   natural optimists
  as the real thing:
is that the way   you worked it?

Did you nuzzle   into the hollow of her hand
and give her courage? And

did you do it for her
dicks, when push came to shove?
Did you give her something to smile at?

Returns

You accepted love, and wore it
as you wore the giver, lightly on your arm
a whole season
before you tired of it
and tried to send it back again
saying you'd changed your mind.

There was a family
where I used to live, notorious
for the same thing. They'd never pay
more than the first instalment
and return the suit, the coat, the expensive car
after the wedding

or the funeral.
People used to point them out
to one another, not to forget
what like they were.
And I'd love to know
what you think you've deserved.

Grim

It bores her rigid.
If you've collected one
whimpering feeble soul
you've collected all of them
and no-one's had an original word to greet her with
since so far back, she doesn't remember.

The kit's a pain too:
it's like something from the Bronze Age.
You would think they'd have some scientific gizmo now
like that odour-hoovering thing she saw on *CSI*
but no. And it's not the budget
allegedly, it's The Tradition.

Even the smallest size of folding sickle
(and that's all she'll carry—anything bigger
spoils the line of her jacket)
takes some maintenance.
If she had all the time back
she's spent in hotel bathrooms with an oilstone...

she won't tell you exactly what she'd do with it
but she's sure she'd think of something.
Meanwhile, her suggestion
of a fishing-net and a jamjar
is what marked her card with the management
or so she heard.
                    Like she cares
reduced to ways of undermining the uniform
—like a schoolkid—to get her through the working day.

A centimetre higher heels than regulation;
second buttons left undone;
scarlet nail extensions; sparkly earrings...
and then, her hair.

The great cascade of Titian curls
she copied off a picture in a magazine
brought down an official reprimand
but you can do a lot with braids: the Wagnerian horned helmet;
the Lizzie Dripping (black bows, she finds,
for maximum impact). And her favourite

the Princess Leia. Nice and warm in winter
and the punters seem to find it
in particularly poor taste.
These are the little victories

that keep her going.
Sad or what

she thinks in a vacant moment
as she stands outside another door
smoking a brand of menthol cigarette
they're always threatening to discontinue.

Clock-watching;
waiting for her moment.

Afterlife

Imagine this:
how Orpheus faked his own death
to be free of words, free of line, free
of the obligation
to have meanings or to dream them
and came back

as a painter. Imagine
how attentively he grinds the colours, each one
uniquely indescribable.
How he hardly dares to whisper
even their names
for fear these words, too, betray him.

How he primes the ground.
How he loads the brush for the first touch
so tenderly, you imagine;
or with stuttering hands, rapacious
to begin again; and paints

—what?
The dark lights he followed under ground
and sees in his sleep yet?
The red and purple splatter of
beasts' viscera and old bones
he gave to wall-eyed madness?

Or the white sky
the yellow fields
the grey road in front of him

and the trees
framing them, stark with angles,
shimmering with their own life.
Silver and brown and gold
and green and free of the obligation
to dance to anyone’s song.

Last act

When the long nights returned, the staff absconded
leaving all the plate and the cutlery
unpolished. Dressed in one of your less-
difficult gowns, you roamed the empty halls
and for the first time
went down to the lower levels

where you opened bottles of apricots
and ate them with your fingers, trying to guess
if the pantry held enough
to last you out, and thinking
—to your own surprise, nostalgically—
of bread, and your bowl of chocolate.

Your diversions failed you one by one.
Ignorant how the lamps lit,
you broke your bobbins making lace
on the terrace under the moonlight
and your spinning-wheel—a toy
of gold and whales' ivory—soon jammed.

The clavier lost its tune;
the books in the library repelled you
with their odour of near decay.
At last there was no more to detain you.

The grooms had taken the horses
when they went—an act of mercy,
since you had no idea how to feed
or saddle the things—so you walked away
wondering if you were too late

to learn about the world.
And for the want of a better instrument,
your last act as a Princess
was to take off one embroidered satin shoe
and use the fine heel
to smash the ice on the fishpond.

Acknowledgements

I would like to thank all the people who have guided and encouraged me in my writing over the years, especially Terry Martin, Esther Read, Sally Evans, Brian Johnstone, and Eleanor Livingstone; and to thank John Bolland and Sheila Wakefield for their advice in shaping this collection.

Poems in this collection have appeared (sometimes in slighty different form) in the following publications/sites: *Agenda; Angle; ARTEMISpoetry; CAMPUS* (The Poetry School); *Gutter; Ink, Sweat and Tears; The Interpreter's House; Meeting Points* (Lemon Tree Writers); *New Writing Scotland; Northwords Now; The Open Mouse; poet and geek; Poetry News; Pushing Out the Boat; Quadrant; Read Raw Featured Poets; The Rialto; riverrun; Smiths Knoll.*

'Afterlife' was a runner-up in the Agenda Poetry Competition 2011; 'Daffodils' was a runner-up in the Cardiff International Poetry Competition 2013; 'The Lapland Woman and the Finland Woman' and 'The Water' were chosen for the Scottish Poetry Library's Best Scottish Poems online anthology for 2014 and 2015 respectively ; 'Night Driver' won second prize in the Second Light Open Poetry Competition 2003 and 'Binding' won second prize in the same competition in 2015.

'Visitors' was part of the installation 'After Livingstone: Poets from Scotland & Africa' in the Town Hall, St Andrews as part of StAnza 2013; 'Powers That Be' was published as a Diehard Press poetry poster in 2016.

I am grateful to the editors and organisations concerned for their support of my work.

A NOTE ON THE TYPE

This book is set in Chronicle, a 'blended Scotch' from the Hoefler & Co digital type foundry in New York. Scotch typefaces were associated originally with the Scottish typefounders Alexander Wilson and William Miller and, for historical reasons, became popular in the United States. Chronicle is a distinguished modern updating of this time-honoured style, highly suited to a variety of text uses including the setting of poetry.